Frozen in Time

Copyright © by Harcourt, Inc.

Printed in Mexico

ISBN-13: 978-0-15-352825-5
ISBN-10: 0-15-352825-7

2 3 4 5 6 7 8 9 10   050   11 10 09 08 07 06

Harcourt
SCHOOL PUBLISHERS

Visit *The Learning Site!* www.harcourtschool.com

Unknown Danger

In A.D. 79, Pompeii (pahm•PAY) was a busy Roman city. More than 10,000 people lived there.

Pompeii was an important center of trade. From its port on the Mediterranean Sea, traders could sail to places as far away as Spain and Egypt. Ships carried olive oil and wine from Pompeii to many towns.

Only about a mile away, though, stood a volcano. Mount Vesuvius (vuh•SOO•vee•uhs) had not erupted in hundreds of years. People thought its active days were over.

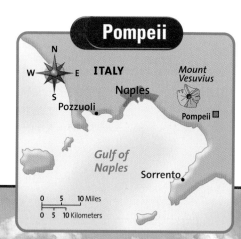

Pompeii

Pompeii was on the Bay of Naples.

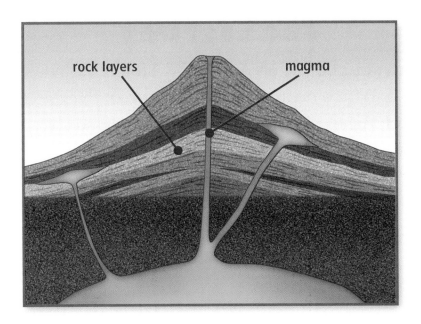

rock layers

magma

But the ground had not been completely quiet. Just 17 years earlier, about the year 62, a powerful earthquake had struck Pompeii. The roofs of buildings caved in. Columns crumbled, and statues fell to the ground. One of the reservoirs broke. It held fresh water for the city. Water flooded the streets. In 79, the city was still repairing some of the damage.

During the earthquake, Mount Vesuvius had rumbled. People were not worried that it might erupt. It had been quiet so long that the sides of the volcano were covered with grass and bushes. Sheep grazed there peacefully.

However, that earthquake had been a warning. The volcano was waking up.

The Last Day

Around 1:00 P.M. on August 24, Mount Vesuvius erupted. With a deafening roar, the top of the volcano blew off. Ashes and hot stones shot thousands of feet into the air. Burning lava ran down the sides of the mountain. Smoke filled the sky. Poisonous fumes filled the air.

That was only the beginning. More explosions followed. Hot ashes from the first eruptions had fallen near Pompeii, but now ashes poured down like thick, hot snow. The city was soon buried in ash.

People tried to escape the eruption.

After the first eruption, many Pompeians tried to escape. Some of them did. Others ran to their cellars, hoping to find safety there. But the poisonous gases reached them. There was no safe place in the city. About 2,000 people died.

Pompeii was buried under 15 feet of ash and rocks. Only a few buildings still stood, their tops poking through the rubble.

In the days that followed, some Pompeians returned to the city. They hoped to find treasures people had left behind. It was a dangerous thing to do. There were still pockets of poisonous gas in the rubble.

Finally, people stopped coming. They understood that Pompeii was gone.

Leaving Pompeii

Pliny was a writer. He lived in Pompeii before the eruption. Pliny wrote about how he and his mother escaped. They walked along the road out of town. Smoke and ash made it too dark to see. They rested by the road. The ashes began to fall harder. "We rose . . . and shook them off. Otherwise, we should have been buried and crushed beneath their weight," he wrote.

Herculaneum was another city destroyed by the eruption.

Hints of the Past

Hundreds of years passed, and people forgot about Pompeii. The only memory of it was a rumor that a lost city lay somewhere near the Bay of Naples. No one knew exactly where.

Then, in 1594, workers found a hint of where the city lay. They were digging a channel to carry water. As they dug, they came across bits and pieces of ruined buildings. No one followed these clues to search for the buried city.

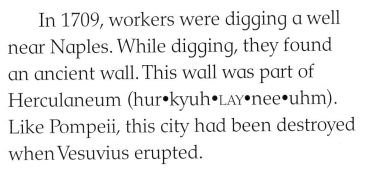

In 1709, workers were digging a well near Naples. While digging, they found an ancient wall. This wall was part of Herculaneum (hur•kyuh•LAY•nee•uhm). Like Pompeii, this city had been destroyed when Vesuvius erupted.

Unlike Pompeii, though, Herculaneum had been buried under a mixture of mud and lava. As it cooled, the mixture became as hard as stone. It was very difficult to dig through it. Workers in the 1700s did not have the technology to break up the stone.

A new town had been built on top of the ruins of old Herculaneum. Excavating, or digging out, the ancient city would have destroyed parts of the newer one. So, after exploring only a little of the old city, the workers stopped.

A statue from Herculaneum

7

Raiding the Past

The discoveries at Herculaneum stirred interest. People began to search for more ruins. In 1763, they found a piece of carved stone. It had the Latin word for Pompeii on it. The lost city had been found.

Soon people were coming from all over to excavate parts of Pompeii. Many of these searchers were not scientists. They were treasure hunters.

They did not follow a careful system. They did not make maps to show what they found and where. Often, they did not care what they ruined as they searched for treasures. Many of the excavators just wanted to carry away the valuable things they found.

Workers at Pompeii

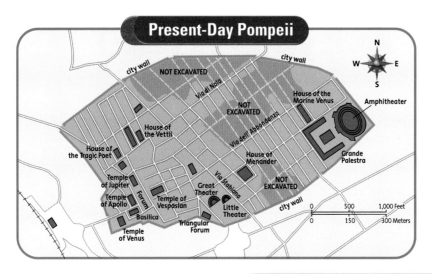

Present-Day Pompeii

city wall

NOT EXCAVATED

city wall

Via di Nola

NOT EXCAVATED

House of the Marine Venus

Amphitheater

House of the Vettii

Via dell' Abbondanza

House of the Tragic Poet

House of Menander

Grande Palestra

Temple of Jupiter

Great Theater

NOT EXCAVATED

Temple of Apollo

Forum

Temple of Vespasian

Via Stabiana

Little Theater

city wall

Basilica

Triangular Forum

Temple of Venus

N W E S

0 500 1,000 Feet
0 150 300 Meters

Scholars needed to know where each object was found. They wanted answers to questions. What kind of building was the object found in? Was it in a temple? Was it in a home? What was the object made of? The answers to such questions were clues to life in Pompeii.

Fiorelli worked hard to uncover Pompeii.

Finally, in 1860, a man named Giuseppe Fiorelli became director of the excavations. Fiorelli was an archaeologist. Archaeologists are scientists who study how people lived in ancient times. As a scientist, Fiorelli was very careful about the way he excavated Pompeii.

A City Shows Itself

Fiorelli wanted to save as much of Pompeii as he could. That way, people could see what it was like before the eruption. His plan was to uncover the whole city, block by block. He kept careful records of each item he and his workers found and where they found it.

Another part of Fiorelli's plan was that the treasures he and his workers found would stay in Pompeii. Valuable things would go into a museum, but the city itself was also a kind of museum. Fiorelli understood that people would have to protect Pompeii.

Fiorelli and his team carefully excavated Pompeii.

People would meet in the Forum.

Just uncovering the buildings was not enough for Fiorelli. He wanted to restore them—to clean them and fix them. He wanted to make them look as much as possible like Roman homes.

Fiorelli also wanted to include the people of Pompeii. The ash that fell on the city had hardened around the bodies of the dead. After all these years, there was nothing left of the bodies.

Fiorelli realized that the hardened ash was like a shell or a mold, with an empty space inside. He poured plaster into the space and let it harden. When he removed the hard ash around the plaster, he found the shape of the body.

What Pompeii Tells Us

Probably the most exciting discoveries in Pompeii were the works of art. The home of a wealthy family might have sculptures, wall paintings, and mosaics.

To make a mosaic, an artist placed small pieces of colored materials right into a wall. Some floors also had mosaics, while others had tiles. Some homes had a mosaic portrait of the owners.

The different styles of art in Pompeii show that many artists worked there. For wealthy Pompeians, art was an important part of their lives. They were willing to spend their money to make their homes beautiful.

This art was buried for thousands of years.

Archaeologists uncovered more secrets of Pompeii. Since the eruptions began around midday, some people were sitting down to lunch. Excavators found a whole meal set out on a table. They found loaves of bread in a bakery oven. From these clues, they got an idea of the foods people ate.

Archaeologists look for information about all people. They want to learn what they can about the lives of the rich and poor, business people and city officials, adults and children, slaves and freed slaves. Even the animals interest them. One house had a mosaic in front with the picture of a guard dog.

The Future of Pompeii

Pompeii has long been a favorite of tourists. Visitors enjoy the art, shops, gardens, and houses. They stop to read the writings on the walls. Outside a house, they read the owner's sign: "No place for loafers here; move along." Maybe they laugh, because they have seen other signs just like it.

For a little while, visitors put themselves in the place of the Pompeians on that terrible day. They stare toward Mount Vesuvius.

Pompeians enjoyed the outdoors.

Tourists cross the streets of Pompeii just like people of Roman times.

The tourists are in little danger. But Pompeii itself may be. For hundreds of years, it was frozen in time, lost to the world. Now, though, it is like any other city. Weather and pollution wear down its buildings.

Mount Vesuvius is still active. The volcano has erupted many times since A.D. 79. New inventions allow scientists to keep watch on changes within a volcano. When they see pressure rising, they know an eruption might take place. They can warn people in the area.

For now, the city that was once lost is protected. Its people and the lives they lived are remembered.

Think and Respond

1. What happened to Pompeii in A.D. 62?

2. How did the eruption affect Herculaneum and Pompeii differently?

3. How did Giuseppe Fiorelli's work differ from that of earlier excavators?

4. What does the presence of so much art in Pompeii tell us about the people who lived there?

5. What threatens Pompeii today?

 # Activity

Imagine that you have a chance to visit Pompeii. Make a travel poster that invites tourists to visit Pompeii.